Coaching for Commitment

SECOND EDITION

• •

Participant Workbook 2

Module Three: Coaching Process 2: Initiating Alternatives

Module Four: Coaching Teams

Dennis C. Kinlaw

Jossey-Bass
Pfeiffer

SAN FRANCISCO

Copyright © 1999 by Jossey-Bass/Pfeiffer

ISBN: 0-7879-4618-4

Printed in the United States of America

Published by

350 Sansome Street, 5th Floor
San Francisco, California 94104-1342
(415) 433-1740; Fax (415) 433-0499
(800) 274-4434; Fax (800) 569-0443

Visit our website at: www.pfeiffer.com

Printing   10   9   8   7   6   5   4   3

This book is printed on acid-free, recycled stock that meets or exceeds the minimum GPO and
EPA requirements for recycled paper.

Contents

• •

• •

Module Four: Coaching Teams

Introduction to Coaching for Commitment

♦ ♦

This workbook contains the third and fourth of four modules intended for use in an integrated, modular skills-training program for leaders and key employees at every level in every kind of organization. This program is based extensively on the second edition of *Coaching for Commitment* by Dennis C. Kinlaw, Ed.D., published by Jossey-Bass/Pfeiffer.

As organizations have become more and more employee-centered and have expected more and more leadership behavior from empowered employees, it has become clear that coaching is a function that *every* member of an organization can and should perform. Both workbooks in this package are built on the assumption that every person at every level in every organization can and should function as a coach.

Coaching works at every level and in all organizational relationships: to improve the performance of individuals (including the top executives of companies); to improve the performance of teams; and, ultimately, to improve the performance of total organizations. It works because coaching helps to create the major factors that lead to commitment. Coaching helps people to clarify their goals and priorities and to understand what is important and what is not. It invites people to demonstrate competent influence over their performance and careers, improves people's knowledge and skills so that they can do their best, and conveys to others just how important and appreciated they are. Coaching also helps people resolve their performance problems and challenges people to ever higher levels of performance.

All of the modules in this training program have been designed to build the necessary competencies required to conduct successful coaching conversations. They are intended to be used in sequence and are carefully designed to move

♦ ♦

participants through the process from learning the basic concepts to mastering the skills required to conduct a complete coaching conversation.

The four modules of the program are listed below:

- Module One: Introduction to Coaching for Commitment
- Module Two: Coaching Process 1: Responding to Needs
- Module Three: Coaching Process 2: Initiating Alternatives
- Module Four: Coaching Teams

Module Three

Coaching Process 2: Initiating Alternatives

Objectives

Module One: Introduction to Coaching for Commitment

- To gain a higher appreciation for the value of coaching as a strategy for improving the performance of co-workers, teams, and the total organization
- To understand the two primary processes that apply to most coaching conversations
- To practice the use of the core skills that support all successful coaching conversations
- To score and interpret the Problem-Solving Skills Questionnaire

Module Two: Coaching Process 1: Responding to Needs

- To review coaching processes and general skills
- To practice use of general skills to develop information in a videotaped interaction and feedback activity
- To score and interpret the Coaching Skills Inventory
- To practice special skills for Coaching Process 1: Responding to Needs
- To practice Coaching Process 1: Responding to Needs in a videotaped interaction and feedback activity

Module Three: Coaching Process 2: Initiating Alternatives

- **To review the core skills that support all successful coaching conversations**
- **To practice special skills for Coaching Process 2: Initiating Alternatives**
- **To practice Stage I: Stating Confrontation**
- **To practice Stage II: Using Reaction to Develop Information**
- **To practice Stage III: Resolving**
- **To practice Coaching Process 2: Initiating Alternatives in a videotaped and feedback activity**

Module Four: Coaching Teams

- To review coaching processes and core skills
- To identify special skills for coaching teams
- To practice the special skills for coaching teams
- To practice team coaching skills in a videotaped interaction and feedback activity

Sequence and Schedule for Module Three

Event	Time
Welcome and Administrative Details	10 minutes
Overview and Objectives for Module Three	8 minutes
Norms for the Workshop	2 minutes
Activity 3.1: Review of Module Two and Preview of Module Three	20 minutes
Debrief Activity 3.1	10 minutes
The Two Processes of Coaching	5 minutes
General Skills	5 minutes
Coaching Process 2: Initiating Alternatives	15 minutes
Activity 3.2: Review of Process 2: Initiating Alternatives	20 minutes
Debrief Activity 3.2	10 minutes
BREAK	10 minutes
Process Stage I: Stating Confrontation	10 minutes
Activity 3.3: Practicing Stage I: Stating Confrontation	25 minutes
Debrief Activity 3.3	10 minutes
Process Stage II: Using Reaction to Develop Information	10 minutes
Activity 3.4: Practicing Stage II: Using Reaction to Develop Information	25 minutes
Debrief Activity 3.4	10 minutes
Process Stage III: Resolving	10 minutes
LUNCH	30 minutes
Activity 3.5: Critique of Video Behavior Model: Process 2: Initiating Alternatives	20 minutes
Debrief Activity 3.5	10 minutes
Activity 3.6: Practice with Process 2: Coaching Examples	30 minutes
Debrief Activity 3.6	10 minutes
BREAK	10 minutes
Activity 3.7: Preparation for Videotaped Interaction and Feedback	15 minutes
Activity 3.8: Practice Videotaped Interaction and Feedback: Process 2: Initiating Alternatives	1 hour, 45 minutes
Debrief Activity 3.8	10 minutes
Review and Action Log	10 minutes
Module Three: Key Learning Points	10 minutes

Norms for the Workshop

- Informal and interactive
- Take one another's comments and questions seriously
- Listen to understand
- Avoid nitpicking
- Focus on skill development
- No side conversations
- Be prompt
- Have fun

Activity 3.1

Review of Module Two
and Preview of Module Three

You have _____ minutes for this activity.

Purposes of Activity

- To review the key learning points from Module Two: Coaching Process 1: Responding to Needs
- To preview the key activities in Module Three: Coaching Process 2: Initiating Alternatives
- To clarify any outstanding issues or questions

Directions

Task 1 Review this activity as a team and ensure that your team understands what tasks it must complete.

Task 2 Select a recorder who will serve as the spokesperson for your team.

Task 3 Work as a team and review the objectives for Module Two and the key learning points from Module Two: Coaching Process 1: Responding to Needs that are repeated below. Record any questions that you may have about the objectives and key learning points. If members are not sure that they have reached the objectives or they are not fully confident about the key learning points, note this information.

Objectives for Module Two: Coaching Process 1: Responding to Needs

- To review coaching processes and general skills
- To practice use of general skills to develop information in a video-taped interaction and feedback activity

- To score and interpret the Coaching Skills Inventory
- To practice special skills for Coaching Process 1: Responding to Needs
- To practice Coaching Process 1 in a videotaped interaction and feed-back activity

Key Learning Points for Module Two

1. The two processes that apply to most coaching conversations are the following:

   - Coaching Process 1: Responding to Needs
   - Coaching Process 2: Initiating Alternatives

2. The general coaching skills that support the two coaching processes are as follows:

   - Attending
   - Acknowledging
   - Probing
   - Reflecting
   - Indicating respect
   - Self-disclosure
   - Immediacy
   - Summarizing

3. The stage-specific skills of Process 1 are as follows:

   Skills for Stage I: Involving

   - Clarifying

   Skills for Stage II: Developing

   - Resourcing
   - Confirming

   Skills for Stage III: Resolving

   - Reviewing
   - Planning
   - Affirming

Comments and Questions:

Task 4   Work as a team and discuss the objectives for Module Three below. Look through the materials included in this workbook. Note any questions that you have about the objectives and what we will be doing.

Objectives for Module Three:
Coaching Process 2: Initiating Alternatives

- To review the core skills that support all successful coaching conversations
- To practice special skills for Coaching Process 2: Initiating Alternatives
- To practice Stage I: Stating Confrontation
- To practice Stage II: Using Reaction to Develop Information
- To practice Stage III: Resolving
- To practice Coaching Process 2: Initiating Alternatives in a video-taped and feedback activity

Comments and Questions:

Task 5   Bring any comments and questions to the general session for discussion.

Coaching Process 1: Responding to Needs

- Counseling

- Mentoring

- Tutoring

Coaching Process 2: Initiating Alternatives

- Confronting

General Skills

Attending: Using nonverbal behavior to communicate and listening without evaluating

Acknowledging: Verbal and nonverbal indications of being involved in the conversation

Probing: Asking questions and directing

Reflecting: Stating in one's own words what the other person has said or is feeling

Indicating respect: Not using behaviors that ridicule, generalize, or judge

Self-disclosure: Indicating that one has had a similar experience

Immediacy: Drawing attention to what is happening in the conversation

Summarizing: Pausing during the conversation to summarize key points

Coaching Process 2: Initiating Alternatives

Goals	Stage-Specific Skills	General Skills (typically useful at all stages)
Process Stage 1: Stating Confrontation		
Reduce resistance Limit topic Establish change focus	*Confronting:* Making a statement that is specific, limited, and future oriented	*Attending:* Using nonverbal behavior to communicate and listening without evaluating *Acknowledging:* Verbal and nonverbal indications of being involved in the conversation *Probing:* Asking questions and directing *Reflecting:* Stating in one's own words what the other person has said or is feeling *Indicating respect:* Not using behaviors that ridicule, generalize, or judge *Self-disclosure:* Indicating that one has had a similar experience *Immediacy:* Drawing attention to what is happening in the conversation *Summarizing:* Pausing in the conversation to summarize key points

Goals	Stage-Specific Skills	General Skills (typically useful at all stages)

Process Stage II: Using Reaction to Develop Information

Goals	Stage-Specific Skills	General Skills (typically useful at all stages)
Defuse resistance Information Insight Problem definition/ causes Causes	*Setting aside one's own agenda:* Mental discipline of focusing on what the other person needs to say and using the general skills to explore fully the other person's point of view	Attending Acknowledging Probing Reflecting Indicating respect Self-disclosure Immediacy Summarizing

Process Stage III: Resolving

Goals	Stage-Specific Skills	General Skills (typically useful at all stages)
Ownership of problem or opportunity Next steps Commitment Positive relationship Closure	*Reviewing:* Going over key points of session to ensure common under-standing *Planning:* Building strategies and agreeing on next steps *Affirming:* Comment-ing on a person's strengths and positive prospects	Attending Acknowledging Probing Reflecting Indicating respect Self-disclosure Immediacy Summarizing

Review of Coaching Process 2: Initiating Alternatives

You have _____ minutes for this activity.

Purposes of Activity

- To review Coaching Process 2: Initiating Alternatives
- To identify anything about the process that requires clarifying

Directions

Task 1   Review this activity as a team and ensure that your team understands what tasks it must complete.

Task 2   Select a recorder who will serve as the spokesperson for your team.

Task 3   Work as a team and review all the stages of Coaching Process 2: Initiating Alternatives on the previous pages. The purpose of this review is to prepare you for using the process in practice videotaped interactions. As you review, note any comments or questions that you have. Bring these to the general session for discussion.

Comments or Questions:

Process Stage I: Stating Confrontation

Goals of Stage I

- To reduce resistance and negative emotions
- To limit coaching topic
- To establish change focus

Stage-Specific Skill: Phrasing the Confrontation

- Be specific
- Limit the problem
- Be future oriented

Activity 3.3

Practicing Stage I: Stating Confrontation

You have _____ minutes for this activity.

Purposes of Activity

- To review the three characteristics of a positive confrontation
- To practice writing positive confrontations that have these three characteristics

Directions

Task 1   Review this activity as a team and ensure that your group understands what tasks must be completed.

Task 2   Select a recorder who will serve as the spokesperson for your team.

Task 3   Work as a team and review the three characteristics of a positive confrontation found below. Ensure that all team members understand these characteristics.

The three characteristics of a positive confrontation are

- Be specific
- Limit the problem
- Be future oriented

Task 4   Work as individuals. Assume that you have decided to confront each of the people described below about a performance problem. For each case, write the words that you would use in stating your confrontation. Remember to be specific, limit the problem, and be future oriented.

Situation 1: Jenkins is a new supervisor you have recently promoted. Jenkins has begun to fall behind in some of the milestones of an office automation project. You have discussed this problem with him or her previously. You noted improvement for awhile, but now Jenkins has started to fall behind again.

Situation 2: A peer of yours has criticized your department in the presence of your boss. You feel the criticism was uncalled for and was in poor taste. You feel that the criticism reflects on you personally and that, at the least, your associate could have made the criticism to you in private. You have arranged a meeting with your associate to repair the damage and ensure that your associate does not repeat this sort of behavior again.

Situation 3: Potter, a fellow team member, has often failed to respond to your phone calls or e-mail messages. The two of you are responsible for producing the master schedule for one of your team's projects, which is to create some enhancements to your company's human resource information system. You have arranged a meeting with Potter to confront him or her about this lack of responsiveness.

Situation 4: You have spoken to Smith on one previous occasion about the quality of his or her technical reports. Smith consistently uses poor grammar and confusing sentence structure. You have called Smith in again because his or her latest report is not acceptable to you.

Situation 5: You feel strongly that your boss is not supporting you in project meetings in which contractors, other departments, and higher management are represented. You feel that your boss leaves you personally out on a limb and shares no responsibility for your work. You have decided to confront your boss on the issue to ask your boss to support you more.

Situation 6: You have a new idea for improving the productivity and performance of your work group. Your boss is not too interested in productivity improvement and you expect him or her to be very unresponsive. But you have decided to take the bull by the horns and present your idea anyway.

Situation 7: You suspect that a colleague has been going behind your back and complaining to your boss that you have not been cooperating on a project that you and your colleague are working on. You feel that you have been cooperating and that, at any rate, your colleague has no business complaining to your boss without coming to you first. You decide to speak to your colleague about the situation.

Task 5   Start with one member of your team and proceed clockwise around the group, with the first person responding to Situation 1 and the second to Situation 2, and so on.

The other team members are to listen and give feedback in answer to the following questions:

- Was the confrontation concrete?
- Did the confrontation limit the problem?
- Was the confrontation future oriented?
- How might the confrontation have been improved?

Continue the process until at least one confrontation has been reviewed for each of the situations.

Task 6   Bring your results from Task 5 to the general session. Your trainer will ask for sample confrontations from each team.

Process Stage II: Using Reaction to Develop Information

- This stage of the process requires more discipline than any other element in coaching.
- When people are confronted about a performance problem, they can be expected to react.
- The guiding principle in confronting a performance problem is, *Don't fight the person's reaction; fix the performance problem.*

Stage II Goals

- Information
- Insight
- Definition of problem or opportunity
- Defuse resistance

Stage II Skills

All of the general skills described in Process I come into play in reaching the goals of Stage II of Process 2: attending, acknowledging, showing respect, probing, etc. These are the skills for using the reaction to a confrontation to develop information. In both processes, Stage II is fully focused on the needs of the persons being coached. The one stage-specific skill for Stage II in Process 2 is the mental skill of setting aside one's own agenda.

Setting aside one's agenda does not mean that the coach forgets all about the problem or opportunity as phrased in Stage I. But coaches cannot focus on the other person and fully explore the other person's reactions and point of view unless they can mentally "let go" of their own definition of the problem or opportunity.

Example

CONFRONTATION: I tried to call the office three times this morning from the field station, and all I got was the answering service. When I am in the field talking to our customers, I badly need to be able to reach this office and talk to a person and get a quick response. Have you got any ideas?

RESPONSE: I can't do everything. I have to leave my desk sometimes, and there isn't anyone else around to cover for me.

NOT SETTING ASIDE: I'm sure that there are a lot of excuses for not covering the phones, but I must insist that they be covered.

SETTING ASIDE: Why don't we start by listing all the problems that you are having, and then see what kind of solutions are most feasible? (open probe)

Activity 3.4

Practicing Stage II:
Using Reaction to Develop Information

You have _____ minutes for this activity.

Purposes of Activity

- To review the goals and skills of Stage II of Coaching Process 2: Initiating Alternatives
- To practice using reaction to develop information

Directions

Task 1   Review this activity as a team and ensure that your group understands what tasks it must complete.

Task 2   Select a recorder who will serve as the spokesperson for your team.

Task 3   Work as a team and review the goals and skills of Stage II.

Task 4   Work as individuals. Assume that the responses given below were made by the people after you confronted them in the previous activity. Practice setting aside your agenda and use either a probing response or a reflecting response to solicit information. If you are unsure what kind of responses these are, discuss your questions with your team members before proceeding.

Situation 1

JENKINS: I've just been having a lot of things happen to me lately. My main problem is that I just can't count on the people who are working for me. I end up doing most of the work myself.

Situation 2

PEER: Listen, I call them the way I see them. If you don't want to be criticized, then carry your part of the job and see that those people who work with you do the same.

Situation 3

POTTER: I can't do my job and stay in the office to answer phone calls. I get back to you as quickly as I get back to anyone else. I'm working on other projects, you know, besides the master schedule. If you really want to get in touch with me, you can.

Situation 4

SMITH: I'm not an English major; I'm an engineer. Like I told you before, we pay secretaries to type reports and put them in the right form.

Situation 5

BOSS: You don't understand the politics of this kind of thing. Those people want to prove they are doing their jobs. The way they do it is to find fault with someone. The other day it was just your turn. The real message was directed at me. They are telling me that I had better keep your feet to the fire. If I defend you, it looks as if I'm trying to sweep something under the rug.

Situation 6

BOSS: All this productivity stuff is simply window dressing. I'm not going to waste the time of our group taking on some bureaucratic nonsense.

Situation 7

COLLEAGUE: I think that you've misread this. I didn't do anything except let the boss know how the project was going. I didn't say anything about your cooperating or not.

Task 5   After team members have written their responses, start with one member of your team and proceed clockwise around the team. The first member is to give his or her reaction to the Response to Situation 1. The other team members are to listen and give feedback in answer to the following questions:

- Was the agenda dropped?
- Was the response a probe or a reflecting response?
- How could the response be improved?

Continue around the group, treating each response in turn until at least one reaction has been reviewed for each of the responses.

Task 6   Select samples of your responses to be discussed during the general session.

Process Stage III: Resolving

Goals of Stage III

The general and overarching goals of all coaching conversations are to obtain *commitment to higher levels of performance, while maintaining positive work relationships* between coach and the person coached. In addition to commitment, Stage III has the following specific goals:

Ownership: Ownership describes the other person's expressed willingness to assume responsibility for "fixing" the problem or for planning to take advantage of a new job opportunity.

Next Steps: The best coaching sessions to improve performance or raise performance to a higher level include some discussion of "next steps," what the person coached will do and how the coach will be kept informed.

Closure: Closure is the goal of ensuring that the person being coached has a sense of completeness. In the case of performance problems, this means that he or she feels fully heard and that exactly what will be done to fix the problem has been identified. The person is not left with the feeling that some intangible or vague problem, such as "being more professional," "being a better team player," or "being more diligent" must be solved. The sense of closure is assured by reviewing what has transpired during the coaching conversation and by affirming the other person's strengths.

Stage III Skills

Reviewing: Reviewing ensures clarity at the end of a conversation in which quite different points of view may have emerged. Reviewing helps achieve the goal of closure. It also encourages a demonstration of the other person's commitment.

Planning: Planning is the skill that identifies next steps, that is, the strategies for resolving the problem or for taking advantage of an improvement opportunity. Planning also includes some way to keep the coach informed of progress. Skilled coaches will develop (with the person being coached) a set of specific actions to solve the problem or take advantage of the chance for greater responsibility.

Affirming: People who have been confronted can easily leave a coaching session with some unresolved negative feelings. It is important that coaches end a confrontation with some positive comments about the other person's strengths. These comments can relate to the general strengths that person has exhibited on the job or relate to the efforts that the person has made during the coaching interaction. The goal, of course, is to leave the other person with the most positive belief in his or her capacity to succeed.

Activity 3.5

Critique of Video Behavior Model: Coaching Process 2: Initiating Alternatives

You have _____ minutes for this activity.

Purposes of Activity

- To critique a video behavior model demonstrating the process and skills of Coaching Process 2: Initiating Alternatives
- To develop further the ability to recognize and use the process and skills of Process 2

Directions

Task 1   Review this activity as a team and ensure that your team understands what tasks it must complete.

Task 2   You will observe a person demonstrating the process and skills of Coaching Process 2: Initiating Alternatives. You are not evaluating the total performance of the person. Your goal is to develop your own ability to identify the stages in Process 2 and the skills typically used during the process.

   Think of the person on the videotape as one of your colleagues in this workshop. When you discuss what you have observed, use your discussion as an opportunity for practicing feedback. Remember that feedback

- Is specific and concrete
- Is descriptive of behavior (what you see and hear)
- Is free of opinion and interpretation
- Offers practical recommendations for improvement

Task 3   Work as a team and review the Activity 3.5 Observation Form. Make sure that each person understands how to use the form and understands the stages and the skills noted on the form.

Task 4   Observe the video model and complete your Observation Form. Once the video is finished, discuss your observations. Note any significant disagreements among team members and try to reconcile these disagreements.

Comments and Questions:

Task 5   Bring the results of your discussion from Task 4 to the general session.

Activity 3.5 Observation Form

Question	Observation	Comment/Examples
1. Was the stated confrontation specific?	Yes No	
2. Did the stated confrontation limit the problem?	Yes No	
3. Was the stated confrontation future oriented?	Yes No	
4. Did the coach drop his or her agenda?	Yes No	
5. Was there a clear transition to Stage II?	Yes No	
6. Did the coach use the following skills in developing information in Stage II?		
Acknowledging	Yes No	
Open probes	Yes No	
Closed probes	Yes No	
Reflecting	Yes No	
Self-disclosure	Yes No	
Immediacy	Yes No	
Summarizing	Yes No	

Activity 3.5 Observation Form (cont.)

Question	Observation		Comment/Examples
7. Was there a clear transition to Stage III?	Yes	No	
8. Did the coach use the following skills in Stage III?			
Reviewing	Yes	No	
Planning	Yes	No	
Affirming	Yes	No	
9. Did the coach develop the other person's ownership of the problem or opportunity?	Yes	No	
10. Was there a follow-up plan?	Yes	No	
11. Did the coach consistently demonstrate respect?	Yes	No	

Activity 3.6

Practice with Coaching Examples

You have _____ minutes for this activity.

Purposes of Activity

- To use written coaching examples to develop further understanding of Coaching Process 2: Initiating Alternatives
- To develop further the skills for using Coaching Process 2

Directions

Task 1   Review this activity as a team and ensure that your team understands what tasks it must complete.

Task 2   Select a recorder who will serve as the spokesperson for your team.

Task 3   Work as a team. Follow the directions below for using the examples of Coaching Process 2 found in *Coaching for Commitment*, pages 115–122.

1. Turn to Example 2: Confronting Unsuccessful Performance on page 118.
2. Cover up the right-hand column of the example.
3. Have one team member serve as the coach and another team member serve as the person being coached.
4. The team members serving as coach and as the person being coached read the script aloud. After each statement the coach makes, the team is to identify the kind of behavior being demonstrated—for example, confrontation, probing, reflecting, acknowledging, summarizing, reviewing, planning, and so on. Record the team's consensus in each case.

5. As the script is read, see whether the team can identify when the process moves from Stage I to Stage II and to Stage III.

6. Check the team's consensus against the book for each response.

Task 4   Work as a team. This time have one team member read the remarks of the person being coached and other team members substitute their own coaching responses for the ones in the book.

Task 5   If directed by your trainer, repeat Tasks 3 and 4 for Example 1: Challenging a Person to Accept a More Complex Job on pages 116–118.

Task 6   Bring any questions that you have about the activity or Process 2 to the general session for discussion.

Comments or Questions:

Activity 3.7

Preparation for
Videotaped Interaction and Feedback

You have _____ minutes for this activity.

Purposes of Activity

- To develop a situation for each person for his or her use during the videotaped interaction and feedback practice that follows
- To review Coaching Process 2: Initiating Alternatives again

Directions

Task 1   Review this activity as a team and ensure that your group understands what tasks it must complete.

Task 2   Work as individuals. You will soon be participating in an activity in which you and your colleagues will practice Process 2: Initiating Alternatives. Create a situation that you can use when coaching one of your teammates, who will act as a colleague being confronted. Complete the outline below.

Describe the person whom you will confront.

- What is the job of the person whom you will confront?

- What is the condition or performance that you want to "fix"?

- What is your relationship to the person you are confronting—that is, peer, subordinate, or boss?

Task 3   If you have any questions about the situation you have created or how the situation will be used, bring these questions to the general session for discussion.

Comments or Questions:

Activity 3.8

Practice with Videotaped Interaction and Feedback: Coaching Process 2: Initiating Alternatives

You have _____ minutes for this activity.

Purposes of Activity

- To practice using Process 2 and its skills in a videotaped interaction
- To obtain feedback about your use of Process 2 and its skills

Directions

Task 1   Review this activity as a team and ensure that your team understands what tasks it must complete.

Task 2   Select a recorder who will serve as the spokesperson for your team.

Task 3   Prepare for the practice interaction that follows by assigning each member of your team a letter.

Designation Letter	Team Member
A	
B	
C	
D	
E	
F	

Task 4   During this practice interaction, each team member will practice using Process 2 and the skills associated with it. Your personal goal is to discipline yourself to use this process and these skills. Each "coach" will explain to a colleague the situation that he or she created in the previous activity. The coach will then confront the person being coached with the performance problem.

Read and be sure that you understand the following information:

During each interaction, one team member will be designated as timer. All members (including the timer) will serve as observers and, at the end of each interaction, will use their Activity 3.8 Observation Forms to give feedback to the member serving as coach. The sequence for the interaction is as follows:

1. Member A (coach) teaches Member B the situation he or she has created.

2. Member A then confronts Member B and conducts the coaching interaction, using Coaching Process 2. The interaction is taped and observers record their observations on the Activity 3.8 Observation Form.

3. The tape is stopped and rewound. The team discusses the interaction and observers use the Activity 3.8 Observation Form to give feedback to the "coach."

4. Selected portions of the tape are replayed for the benefit of the person who acted as coach.

5. Repeat sequence outlined in Steps 1 through 4 until each member has functioned as the coach.

Time per Round

Seven minutes for interaction; five minutes for feedback; four minutes to replay portions of the tape.

Task 5   Follow the schedule on the next page to complete your round of practice interactions. The letter with the asterisk denotes the timer for each round. *Timers:* Stop each interaction *exactly* at the end of seven minutes.

Presenter	Responder	Observer/Timer
A	B	C, D, E, F*
B	C	D, E, F, A*
C	D	E, F, A, B*
D	E	F, A, B, C*
E	F	A, B, C, D*
F	A	B, C, D, E*

Task 6   Discuss the activity as a group and identify three key learning points. What did you learn from doing the activity? What would you like to remember? Bring your three key learning points to the general session for discussion.

Comments and Questions:

Activity 3.8 Observation Form

Person Observed: _____

Question	Observation		Comment/Examples
1. Was the stated confrontation specific?	Yes	No	
2. Did the stated confrontation limit the problem?	Yes	No	
3. Was the stated confrontation future oriented?	Yes	No	
4. Did the coach drop his or her agenda?	Yes	No	
5. Was there a clear transition to Stage II?	Yes	No	
6. Did the coach use the following skills in developing information in Stage II?			
Acknowledging	Yes	No	
Open probes	Yes	No	
Closed probes	Yes	No	
Reflecting	Yes	No	
Self-disclosure	Yes	No	
Immediacy	Yes	No	
Summarizing	Yes	No	

Activity 3.8 Observation Form (cont.)

Question	Observation	Comment/Examples
7. Was there a clear transition to Stage III?	Yes No	
8. Did the coach use the following skills in Stage III?		
Reviewing	Yes No	
Planning	Yes No	
Affirming	Yes No	
9. Did the coach develop the other person's ownership of the problem or opportunity?	Yes No	
10. Was there a follow-up plan?	Yes No	
11. Did the coach consistently demonstrate respect?	Yes No	

Activity 3.8 Observation Form

Person Observed: _____

Question	Observation		Comment/Examples
1. Was the stated confrontation specific?	Yes	No	
2. Did the stated confrontation limit the problem?	Yes	No	
3. Was the stated confrontation future oriented?	Yes	No	
4. Did the coach drop his or her agenda?	Yes	No	
5. Was there a clear transition to Stage II?	Yes	No	
6. Did the coach use the following skills in developing information in Stage II?			
Acknowledging	Yes	No	
Open probes	Yes	No	
Closed probes	Yes	No	
Reflecting	Yes	No	
Self-disclosure	Yes	No	
Immediacy	Yes	No	
Summarizing	Yes	No	

Activity 3.8 Observation Form (cont.)

Question	Observation	Comment/Examples
7. Was there a clear transition to Stage III?	Yes No	
8. Did the coach use the following skills in Stage III?		
Reviewing	Yes No	
Planning	Yes No	
Affirming	Yes No	
9. Did the coach develop the other person's ownership of the problem or opportunity?	Yes No	
10. Was there a follow-up plan?	Yes No	
11. Did the coach consistently demonstrate respect?	Yes No	

Activity 3.8 Observation Form

Person Observed: _____

Question	Observation		Comment/Examples
1. Was the stated confrontation specific?	Yes	No	
2. Did the stated confrontation limit the problem?	Yes	No	
3. Was the stated confrontation future oriented?	Yes	No	
4. Did the coach drop his or her agenda?	Yes	No	
5. Was there a clear transition to Stage II?	Yes	No	
6. Did the coach use the following skills in developing information in Stage II?			
Acknowledging	Yes	No	
Open probes	Yes	No	
Closed probes	Yes	No	
Reflecting	Yes	No	
Self-disclosure	Yes	No	
Immediacy	Yes	No	
Summarizing	Yes	No	

Activity 3.8 Observation Form (cont.)

Question	Observation		Comment/Examples
7. Was there a clear transition to Stage III?	Yes	No	
8. Did the coach use the following skills in Stage III?			
Reviewing	Yes	No	
Planning	Yes	No	
Affirming	Yes	No	
9. Did the coach develop the other person's ownership of the problem or opportunity?	Yes	No	
10. Was there a follow-up plan?	Yes	No	
11. Did the coach consistently demonstrate respect?	Yes	No	

Activity 3.8 Observation Form

Person Observed: _____

Question	Observation	Comment/Examples
1. Was the stated confrontation specific?	Yes No	
2. Did the stated confrontation limit the problem?	Yes No	
3. Was the stated confrontation future oriented?	Yes No	
4. Did the coach drop his or her agenda?	Yes No	
5. Was there a clear transition to Stage II?	Yes No	
6. Did the coach use the following skills in developing information in Stage II?		
Acknowledging	Yes No	
Open probes	Yes No	
Closed probes	Yes No	
Reflecting	Yes No	
Self-disclosure	Yes No	
Immediacy	Yes No	
Summarizing	Yes No	

Activity 3.8 Observation Form (cont.)

Question	Observation		Comment/Examples
7. Was there a clear transition to Stage III?	Yes	No	
8. Did the coach use the following skills in Stage III?			
Reviewing	Yes	No	
Planning	Yes	No	
Affirming	Yes	No	
9. Did the coach develop the other person's ownership of the problem or opportunity?	Yes	No	
10. Was there a follow-up plan?	Yes	No	
11. Did the coach consistently demonstrate respect?	Yes	No	

Activity 3.8 Observation Form

Person Observed: _____

Question	Observation		Comment/Examples
1. Was the stated confrontation specific?	Yes	No	
2. Did the stated confrontation limit the problem?	Yes	No	
3. Was the stated confrontation future oriented?	Yes	No	
4. Did the coach drop his or her agenda?	Yes	No	
5. Was there a clear transition to Stage II?	Yes	No	
6. Did the coach use the following skills in developing information in Stage II?			
Acknowledging	Yes	No	
Open probes	Yes	No	
Closed probes	Yes	No	
Reflecting	Yes	No	
Self-disclosure	Yes	No	
Immediacy	Yes	No	
Summarizing	Yes	No	

Activity 3.8 Observation Form (cont.)

Question	Observation	Comment/Examples
7. Was there a clear transition to Stage III?	Yes No	
8. Did the coach use the following skills in Stage III?		
Reviewing	Yes No	
Planning	Yes No	
Affirming	Yes No	
9. Did the coach develop the other person's ownership of the problem or opportunity?	Yes No	
10. Was there a follow-up plan?	Yes No	
11. Did the coach consistently demonstrate respect?	Yes No	

Review and Action Log

Record below the learning points and insights you gained from this module. Next, record ways that you might begin to apply your learning and insights and ways that you can continue to practice what you have learned. Then review "Module Three: Key Learning Points" on the page that follows the worksheet.

Learning Points/Insights	Plans for Practice and Use

Module Three: Key Learning Points

1. Coaching Process 1: Responding to Needs and Coaching Process 2: Initiating Alternatives both proceed through three interdependent stages.

2. Both Process 1 and Process 2 employ a set of general skills for developing information: attending, acknowledging, probing, reflecting, indicating respect, self-disclosure, immediacy, and summarizing.

3. Process 2 applies to those situations in which a coach wants to challenge another person to a higher level of responsibility or performance and to those situations in which a coach wants to remedy a performance problem.

4. The three stages of Coaching Process 2: Initiating Alternatives and their goals are

   • Stage I: Stating the Confrontation: to reduce resistance, limit the topic, and establish a change focus

   • Stage II: Using the Reaction to Develop Information: to defuse resistance, gather information, share insights, and define the problem and its causes

   • Stage III: Resolving: to determine ownership of problem or opportunity and the next steps, obtain a commitment to act, establish a positive relationship, and reach closure

5. In Stage I: Stating the Confrontation, the special skill required is to state the confrontation so that it is specific, limits the problem, and is future oriented (that is, focused on change).

6. In Stage II: Using Reaction to Develop Information, the special skill required is the ability to drop one's agenda and use the general skills to respond to the other person's reactions.

7. Confronting a performance problem is quite different from criticizing behavior or performance. Confrontation is a positive process that focuses on a problem and on creating change. Criticism is a negative process that focuses on a person and on establishing blame.

Module Three: Key Learning Points

1. Coaching Process 1: Responding to Needs and Coaching Process 2: Initiating Alternatives both proceed through three interdependent stages.

2. Both Process 1 and Process 2 employ a set of general skills for developing information: attending, acknowledging, probing, reflecting, indicating respect, self-disclosure, immediacy, and summarizing.

3. Process 2 applies to those situations in which a coach wants to challenge another person to a higher level of responsibility or performance and to those situations in which a coach wants to remedy a performance problem.

4. The three stages of Coaching Process 2: Initiating Alternatives and their goals are

   • Stage I: Stating the Confrontation: to reduce resistance, limit the topic, and establish a change focus

   • Stage II: Using the Reaction to Develop Information: to defuse resistance, gather information, share insights, and define the problem and its causes

   • Stage III: Resolving: to determine ownership of problem or opportunity and the next steps, obtain a commitment to act, establish a positive relationship, and reach closure

5. In Stage I: Stating the Confrontation, the special skill required is to state the confrontation so that it is specific, limits the problem, and is future oriented (that is, focused on change).

6. In Stage II: Using Reaction to Develop Information, the special skill required is the ability to drop one's agenda and use the general skills to respond to the other person's reactions.

7. Confronting a performance problem is quite different from criticizing behavior or performance. Confrontation is a positive process that focuses on a problem and on creating change. Criticism is a negative process that focuses on a person and on establishing blame.

Module Four

· ·

Coaching Teams

Objectives

··

Module One: Introduction to Coaching for Commitment

- To gain a higher appreciation for the value of coaching as a strategy for improving the performance of co-workers, teams, and the total organization
- To understand the two primary processes that apply to most coaching conversations
- To practice the use of the core skills that support all successful coaching conversations
- To score and interpret the Problem-Solving Skills Questionnaire

Module Two: Coaching Process 1: Responding to Needs

- To review coaching processes and general skills
- To practice use of general skills to develop information in a videotaped interaction and feedback activity
- To practice special skills for Coaching Process 1: Responding to Needs
- To score and interpret the Coaching Skills Inventory
- To practice Coaching Process 1: Responding to Needs in a videotaped interaction and feedback activity

Module Three: Coaching Process 2: Initiating Alternatives

- To review the core skills that support all successful coaching conversations
- To practice special skills for Coaching Process 2: Initiating Alternatives
- To practice Stage I: Stating Confrontation
- To practice Stage II: Using Reaction to Develop Information
- To practice Stage III: Resolving
- To practice Coaching Process 2: Initiating Alternatives in a videotaped and feedback activity

··

Module Four: Coaching Teams

- **To review coaching processes and core skills**
- **To identify special skills for coaching teams**
- **To practice the special skills for coaching teams**
- **To practice team coaching skills in a videotaped interaction and feedback activity**

··

Sequence and Schedule for Module Four

Event	Time
Welcome and Administrative Details	10 minutes
Overview and Objectives for Module Four	8 minutes
Norms for the Workshop	2 minutes
Activity 4.1: Review of Module Three and Preview of Module Four	20 minutes
Debrief Activity 4.1	10 minutes
Process 1 and General Skills	10 minutes
Special Skills for Coaching Teams	10 minutes
Skills to Help Teams Manage the Conditions for Effective Team Meetings	15 minutes
Activity 4.2: Understanding and Practicing the Knowledge and Skills to Help Teams Structure Themselves for Effective Team Meetings	45 minutes
Debrief Activity 4.2	10 minutes
BREAK	10 minutes
Skills to Manage Interactions Among Team Members	15 minutes
Activity 4.3: Understanding and Practicing Skills to Manage Interactions Among Team Members	30 minutes
Debrief Activity 4.3	10 minutes
Basics of Team Problem Solving and Decision Making	10 minutes
Activity 4.4: Understanding and Practicing a Structured Problem-Solving Process	30 minutes
Debrief Activity 4.4	10 minutes
LUNCH	30 minutes
Activity 4.5: Understanding and Practicing Opportunity Analysis	30 minutes
Debrief Activity 4.5	10 minutes
Activity 4.6: Critique of Video Team Coaching Behavior Model: Process 1: Responding to Needs	20 minutes
Debrief Activity 4.6	10 minutes
BREAK	10 minutes
Activity 4.7: Practice Team Coaching with Process 1: Responding to Needs	1 hour, 45 minutes
Debrief Activity 4.7	10 minutes
Review and Action Log	10 minutes
Module Four: Key Learning Points	10 minutes

Norms for the Workshop

- Informal and interactive
- Take one another's comments and questions seriously
- Listen to understand
- Avoid nitpicking
- Focus on skill development
- No side conversations
- Be prompt
- Have fun

Activity 4.1

Review of Module Three
and Preview of Module Four

You have _____ minutes for this activity.

Purposes of Activity

- To review the key learning points from Module Three: Coaching Process 2: Initiating Alternatives
- To preview the key activities in Module Four: Coaching Teams
- To clarify any outstanding issues or questions

Directions

Task 1   Review this activity as a team and ensure that your team understands what tasks it must complete.

Task 2   Select a recorder who will serve as the spokesperson for your team.

Task 3   Work as a team and review the objectives for Module Three and the key learning points from Module Three: Coaching Process 2: Initiating Alternatives that are listed below. Record any questions that you may have about the objectives and key learning points. Also, if members are not sure that they have reached the objectives or if they are not fully confident about the key learning points, note this information for later discussion.

Objectives for Module Three:
Coaching Process 2: Initiating Alternatives

- To review the core skills that support all successful coaching conversations
- To practice special skills for Coaching Process 2: Initiating Alternatives
- To practice Stage I: Stating Confrontation

- To practice Stage II: Using Reaction to Develop Information
- To practice Stage III: Resolving
- To practice Coaching Process 2: Initiating Alternatives in a video-taped and feedback activity

Key Learning Points for Module Three

1. Coaching Process 1: Responding to Needs and Coaching Process 2: Initiating Alternatives both proceed through three interdependent stages.

2. Both Process 1 and Process 2 employ a set of general skills for developing information: attending, acknowledging, probing, reflecting, indicating respect, self-disclosure, immediacy, and summarizing.

3. Process 2 applies to those situations in which a coach wants to challenge another person to a higher level of responsibility or performance and to those situations in which a coach wants to remedy a performance problem.

4. The three stages of Coaching Process 2: Initiating Alternatives and their goals are

   - Stage I: Stating the Confrontation: to reduce resistance, limit the topic, and establish a change focus
   - Stage II: Using the Reaction to Develop Information: to defuse resistance, gather information, share insights, and define the problem and its causes
   - Stage III: Resolving: to determine ownership of problem or opportunity and the next steps, obtain a commitment to act, establish a positive relationship, and reach closure

5. In Stage I: Stating Confrontation, the special skill required is to state the confrontation so that it is specific, limits the problem, and is future oriented (that is, focused on change).

6. In Stage II: Using Reaction to Develop Information, the special skill required is the ability to drop one's agenda and use the general skills to respond to the other person's reactions and to develop information.

7. Confronting a performance problem is quite different from criticizing behavior or performance. Confrontation is a positive process that focuses on a problem and on creating change. Criticism is a negative process that focuses on a person and on establishing blame.

Comments and Questions:

Task 4   Work as a team and discuss the objectives for Module Four listed below. Review Coaching Process 1 on pages 60–61. Note any questions that you have about the objectives or about the coaching process and what we will be doing.

Objectives for Module Four: Coaching Teams

- To review coaching processes and core skills
- To identify special skills for coaching teams
- To practice the special skills for coaching teams
- To practice team coaching skills in a videotaped interaction and feedback activity

Comments and Questions:

Task 5 Bring your comments and questions to the general session for discussion.

Coaching Process 1: Responding to Needs

Goals	Stage-Specific Skills	General Skills (typically useful at all stages)
Process Stage 1: Involving		
Clear expectations	*Clarifying:* Establishing the objectives	*Attending:* Using nonverbal behavior to communicate and listening without evaluating
Comfort		
Trust		*Acknowledging:* Verbal and nonverbal indications of being involved in the conversation
		Probing: Asking questions and directing
		Reflecting: Stating in one's own words what the other person has said or is feeling
		Indicating respect: Not using behaviors that ridicule, generalize, or judge
		Self-disclosure: Indicating that one has had a similar experience
		Immediacy: Drawing attention to what is happening in the conversation
		Summarizing: Pausing in the conversation to summarize key points

Goals	Stage-Specific Skills	General Skills (typically useful at all stages)

Process Stage II: Developing

Goals	Stage-Specific Skills	General Skills
Information	*Resourcing:* Providing information, advice, instruction, demonstration, or referral	Attending
Insight		Acknowledging
Problem definition/causes		Probing
	Confirming: Ensuring that results of conversation are mutually understood	Reflecting
Learning		Indicating respect
		Self-disclosure
		Immediacy
		Summarizing

Process Stage III: Resolving

Goals	Stage-Specific Skills	General Skills
Resolution	*Reviewing:* Going over key points of session to ensure common understanding	Attending
Next steps		Acknowledging
Commitment		Probing
	Planning: Building strategies and agreeing on next steps	Reflecting
Positive relationship		Indicating respect
Closure		Self-disclosure
	Affirming: Commenting on a person's strengths and positive prospects	Immediacy
		Summarizing

General Skills

Attending: Using nonverbal behavior to communicate and listening without evaluating

Acknowledging: Verbal and nonverbal indications of being involved in the conversation

Probing: Asking questions and directing

Reflecting: Stating in one's own words what the other person has said or is feeling

Indicating respect: Not using behaviors that ridicule, generalize, or judge

Self-disclosure: Indicating that one has had a similar experience

Immediacy: Drawing attention to what is happening in the conversation

Summarizing: Pausing during the conversation to summarize key points

Special Skills for Coaching Teams

- Knowledge and skills to help teams manage the conditions for effective team meetings
- Knowledge and skills to manage interactions among team members
- Knowledge and skills to help teams use the basics of team problem solving and decision making

Skills to Help Teams Manage the Conditions for Effective Team Meetings

Team coaching requires that coaches have the knowledge and skill

- To help teams structure their meetings so that full use is made of the competencies of team members and so that meetings are conducted with maximum effectiveness and efficiency

- To help team members interact during a meeting in ways that further the team's potential to perform its tasks and reach its goals

Activity 4.2

Understanding and Practicing the Knowledge and Skills to Help Teams Structure Themselves for Effective Team Meetings

You have _____ minutes for this activity.

Purposes of Activity

- To understand the conditions for effective team meetings
- To practice the skills for helping teams manage the conditions for effective team meetings

Directions

Task 1   Review this activity as a team and ensure that your team understands what tasks it must complete.

Task 2   Select a recorder who will serve as the spokesperson for your team.

Task 3   Work as individuals and review the description below of the Elements for Structuring Effective Team Meetings. As you read, note any comments or questions that you may have.

Elements for Structuring Effective Team Meetings

- Ensuring the team develops and uses a clear set of norms to govern how members interact
- Ensuring that the team is always clear and conscious of its tasks and goals

Developing and Using Norms

Structure describes everything that a team does to determine what is expected of team members during a meeting. Structuring a team does not mean setting up the sorts of rules that one might use in large meetings or with groups that are not teams. The success of team meetings depends on maintaining a balance between freedom and control. Structuring a team meeting means helping a team conduct its meetings in a purposeful, rational, and fully conscious manner—while making full use of the mental resources of all team members. Structuring a team should never mean avoiding disagreement or conflict. The most creative results of teams are often produced by playing alternatives against one another.

Norms are listed first, not because norms are more important than tasks, objectives, and goals, but because teams that are not clear about what they intend to do can never be teams in fact. They remain groups of people, but they can never be teams. Teams always perform real work, and superior teams are always quite clear what this work is. Having norms helps raise the potential of teams by strengthening their capacity to perform their tasks and reach their objectives and goals.

Norms set explicit expectations about the behavior of team members before, during, and after a meeting. Norms largely accomplish two things: (1) set responsibilities, and (2) establish communication standards.

To ensure that norms affect team performance, they must be written. Until they have become second nature for members, they should also be visible during meetings, displayed on a flip chart or in some other way.

Norms that set expectations about communication might state that each team member will

- Listen and make sure that he or she has understood what other members mean before speaking
- Pay careful attention to how much each person talks, and ensure that there is a balanced interaction among members
- Never discount or ridicule what other members say
- Consistently speak to the task the team is performing
- Summarize periodically what has been said during a meeting
- Help others make a contribution
- Be candid and always express his or her own mind and opinion
- Be concrete and factual

Helping teams establish norms for their meetings, helping them actively use the norms to structure their meetings, helping them use the norms in real time to adjust team performance, and helping them use their norms to assess their performance can all be intended outcomes of team coaching. An intervention a team coach might make to help a team set norms might sound like this:

- "We are losing a lot of information because some of us are talking at the same time and we are not listening to each other as well as we might. I would like for us to set some guidelines about the way we expect to communicate when we meet."

If a team has set its norms, but during a meeting it is not adhering to these norms, a coach might make the following intervention:

- "We have a norm that states that no person will monopolize the conversation. It seems to me that is exactly what has been happening for the last fifteen minutes."

Comments and Questions:

Tasks, Objectives, and Goals

A second condition that affects a team's structure during a meeting is whether the team is clear about what it is doing and what it intends to produce. Clarifying what a team is doing and what it intends to accomplish does not mean that a team will not go off course. If, however, members keep before the team what it is doing and what it has set out to do, the team must consciously choose to deviate from what it set out to do.

The key word here is "consciously." Teams, like individuals, can become quite oblivious about what they are doing at any one time. One factor in structuring teams is that members be clear about their tasks, objectives, and goals. But structuring teams also means keeping members continuously aware of what they are doing, that is, conscious of their performance. When persons take the initiative to coach a team and bring it back on track, they might say something like the following:

- "When we started this meeting we agreed that we would make a decision about how we would manage our travel funds. We seem to have gotten off on another subject. I suggest we decide now whether we want to work on the travel funds problem and decide how we will manage the funds or whether we want to leave that subject and work on some other problem."

- "We set up this meeting to decide how we would measure our team's performance. For the past ten minutes we have been debating whether or not our performance could be measured. I suggest that we settle what we are here to do. Are we here to establish a set of measures, or are we here to debate whether or not we can measure our performance?"

Comments and Questions:

Task 4   Work as a team and review the Elements in Structuring Effective Team Meetings described above. As you discuss the elements, list the negative consequences that may occur when someone does not step up to coach the team and help it set norms and stay focused on its tasks, objectives, and goals.

Negative Consequences:

Task 5 Bring any unresolved questions about the Elements in Structuring Effective Team Meetings to the general session.

Task 6 Now, you will conduct an activity to use what you have learned and see its importance. Read the following instructions carefully.

Instructions for Team Members

In this activity, you are a special quality improvement team in a large all-purpose store that sells everything from cheese to pillowcases. Each member takes a specific position or role—for example, an employee from gardening, or from menswear, or from toys, checkout, or the stockroom. The purpose of your meeting is to improve customer satisfaction. During the practice session, be yourselves and do not act or pretend that you are someone else. Designate one of your members as a shift supervisor to lead the meeting. Designate one member (other than the designated leader) who is to emerge as the coach during the team meeting, and also appoint a timer. Assume that this is the quality improvement team's first meeting. Make no attempt to bring order out of chaos yourself. At the end of the practice interaction, complete the Activity 4.2 Observation Form.

Instructions for Designated Coach

At an appropriate point in the interaction, try to help the team to establish a set of norms to govern the way it will interact and do business. Although there is one designated coach for this activity, the goal is for everyone to identify how they might help a team develop and use a set of meeting norms.

Instructions for Timer

Stop the interaction at the designated time. During the session, complete the Activity 4.2 Observation Form while observing the designated coach in action. At the end of the practice interaction, lead the feedback discussion, using the Activity 4.2 Observation Form.

Task 7 Use the schedule below and begin the activity.

1. Conduct practice interaction. *Timer:* Limit interaction to *exactly* ten minutes.
2. Timer and members complete Activity 4.2 Observation Form.
3. Timer leads five-minute discussion based on the Activity 4.2 Observation Form.

Activity 4.2 Observation Form

Record your observations and comments below.

1. What was happening when the coach intervened and proposed that the team needed to develop norms?

2. What did the coach do to help the team understand the need for norms? If you had been the coach, what would you have done differently?

3. What norms were developed?

Activity 4.2 Observation Form (cont.)

4. Were the norms concrete? If you had been the coach, what would you have done differently?

_____

5. How well did the coach involve the whole team in developing the norms? If you had been the coach, what would you have done differently?

_____

6. How well did the coach keep the team focused on the task of developing its norms? If you had been the coach, what would you have done differently?

Task 8 Discuss the activity as a team and identify three key learning points. What did you learn from doing the activity? What would you like to remember to help you coach a team and help it develop norms? Post your key learning points on flip-chart paper and bring them to the general session for discussion.

Skills to Manage Interactions Among Team Members

Coaching team members to improve their communication process requires the following special skills:

- Helping team members build on one another's input
- Testing to ensure understanding
- Keeping all members involved

Activity 4.3

Understanding and Practicing Skills
to Manage Interactions Among Team Members

You have _____ minutes for this activity.

Purposes of Activity

- To understand the skills coaches require to manage interactions among team members
- To practice the skills for managing interactions among team members

Directions

Task 1   Review this activity as a team and ensure that your team understands what tasks it must complete.

Task 2   Select a recorder who will serve as the spokesperson for your team.

Task 3   Work as individuals and review the description below of Skills to Manage Interactions Among Team Members. As you read, note any comments or questions that you may have.

Skills to Manage Interactions Among Team Members

Managing communication during a coaching session with a team begins, of course, with mastery of the two processes and skills of Coaching Process 1 and Coaching Process 2. Communicating with a team, however, requires additional knowledge about how to interact with more than one person at a time. The special competencies required include

- Helping team members build on one another's input
- Testing to ensure understanding
- Keeping all members involved

Building on One Another's Input

When teams are not sufficiently disciplined during meetings, they will often not take into account what each member says and fail to develop information systematically, thus not using the full resources of the team. Member A will say something, Member B will ignore what Member A said and make a comment, Member C will ignore what both A and B said and give input, and so on. As the team continues in its interaction, what A, B, C, and other members have said will be forgotten and go unused. Members of teams who accept the function of coach will intervene to help the team build on the input of its members and not ignore that input.

Comments and Questions:

Testing to Ensure Understanding

Coaches can test for understanding at any point in a team's process by phrasing in their own words what they think the team has done up to that point, or coaches may ask team members to restate in their own words what has just been said or summarize what has been covered up to some point in the meeting. Another way to test for understanding is for coaches to give examples to illustrate some point or concept or to ask someone else to give examples.

Coaches can also test for understanding by making connections among the inputs made or helping team members make such connections. A coach might give input like the following:

- "If the team decides to measure and reduce the costs to deliver a service call, how will that impact customer satisfaction?"
- "We've decided to develop operating procedures for our service team. That's going to take time. How will we be able to maintain our current levels of service, if we have to spend so much time organizing ourselves?"

- "We've identified at least three causes for the delay in response time. Do you think that these causes are all different, or do they all come down to the same thing?"

Comments and Questions:

Keeping All Members Involved

Coaching a team means coaching *all* the members of a team. Involvement is not merely desirable socially, but is absolutely necessary for the team to do its best work. For team learning to take place, every team member must learn what is required. For a team to solve a problem and use all of its mental resources in the process, *all* the team members must be involved. For a team to continue to develop as a team and ensure that everyone feels fully included in the team, then *all* members must be involved.

Comments and Questions:

Task 4   Work as a team and review the Skills to Manage Interactions Among Team Members on page 73. As you discuss the skills, list the negative consequences that may occur when no team member steps up to coach the team and help members communicate.

Negative Consequences:

Task 5 Bring any unresolved questions that you have regarding the Skills to Manage Interactions Among Team Members to the general session for discussion.

Task 6 Read the following instructions carefully.

Instructions for Team Members

For the purpose of this activity, you are members of a small cleaning organization that contracts with the owners and managers of office buildings in the inner city to clean offices and remove trash. You are faced with the loss of one of your most important contracts. If you do not obtain new business quickly, some of the team members must be laid off. Put in your own ideas freely. Make no attempt to bring order out of chaos. At the end of the practice interaction, complete the Activity 4.3 Observation Form. Designate one of your members to be the owner of the organization and to lead the meeting. Also designate one member (other than the designated leader) who will emerge as the coach and appoint a timer.

Instructions for Designated Coach

At an appropriate point during the interaction, encourage the team to establish a set of norms to govern the way it will interact and do business. Although there is one designated coach in this activity, the goal is for everyone to identify how they might help a team develop and use a set of meeting norms. Your goal as coach is to help team members interact successfully by using the special skills described earlier: helping team members build on one another's input, testing to ensure understanding, and keeping all members involved.

Instructions for Timer

During the practice session, stop the interaction at the designated time. During the interaction, complete the Activity 4.3 Observation Form while observing the designated coach in action. At the end of the practice interaction, lead the feedback discussion, using the Activity 4.3 Observation Form.

Task 7   Use the sequence below and conduct the activity.

1. Conduct practice interaction. *Timer:* Limit the interaction to *exactly* ten minutes.
2. Timer and members complete the Activity 4.3 Observation Form.
3. Timer leads a five-minute discussion based on the Activity 4.3 Observation Form.

Task 8   Discuss the activity as a team and identify three key learning points. What did you learn from doing the activity? What would you like to remember to help you coach a team and help members interact with one another and with you? Put your key learning points on flip-chart paper and bring them to the general session for further discussion.

Activity 4.3 Observation Form

● ●

Record your observations and comments below.

1. What was happening when the coach intervened and began to try to help the interactions among team members?

2. What did the coach do to help team members build on one another's input? If you had been the coach, what would you have done differently?

3. What did the coach do to ensure understanding? If you had been the coach, what would you have done differently?

4. What did the coach do to keep all members involved? If you had been the coach, what would you have done differently?

Basics of Team Problem Solving and Decision Making

- Structured problem-solving process
- Opportunity analysis
- Brainstorming
- Nominal group technique

Understanding and Practicing a Structured Problem-Solving Process

You have _____ minutes for this activity.

Purposes of Activity

- To understand a basic structured problem-solving process
- To practice the skills for using a basic structured problem-solving process

Directions

Task 1   Review this activity as a team and ensure that your team understands what tasks it must complete.

Task 2   Select a recorder who will serve as the spokesperson for your team.

Task 3   Work as individuals and review the description of a structured problem-solving process below. As you read, note any comments or questions that you may have.

Structured Problem-Solving Process

Two questions confront teams: (1) how to fix what is broken, and (2) how to improve what is not broken. To answer either of these questions, teams must proceed through an orderly and sequential definition of the problem or opportunity and then devise various strategies for solving the problem or taking advantage of the opportunity. The actual steps that teams go through can be conceptualized in a variety of ways, starting with the simple and proceeding to the more complex. A simple five-step process is outlined below that will help coaches to help their teams identify and solve problems or take advantage of opportunities.

1. *Acknowledge that a problem or opportunity exists.* Customer complaints, costs overruns, slips in schedule, and breakdowns in production machines are some of the many *problems* that can be imposed on a team. *Opportunities* to be embraced can include making happy customers even happier, reducing the variance in products more than the required quality limits, or deciding to increase the efficiency and reliability of some work system that is already performing well. The first step is for the team to accept that there is a problem or opportunity.

Comments and Questions:

2. *Collect data.* Next the team must describe the problem or opportunity in quantitative terms. Suppose you were on a team that was responsible for improving a project management training program. You would need data on the following: (1) whether participants were learning what was taught; (2) whether participants were learning what they needed to know; (3) whether participants retained and applied what they learned; and (4) whether they could apply what they knew to improve the performance of their projects.

Comments and Questions:

3. *Identify causes of the problem or the opportunity.* Referring again to the example of the project management training program, suppose you discovered that participants were not learning what they needed to know. The next step would be to find out why they were not learning. The team could use many techniques, such as cause-and-effect diagrams or a simple process of "Why?" analysis. Every time a possible cause for not learning was identified, they could simply ask, "Why?" When the answer to that question was identified, the group would again ask, "Why?" until they identified the root causes.

Comments and Questions:

4. *Identify possible solutions.* Solutions are strategies to solve problems or to improve some aspect of performance. Teams can test the appropriateness of a solution by specifying the payoffs that the solution would produce. For example, we might propose that a set of objectives on pocket-sized cards be made for each participant and that before and after each session, participants be asked to use their cards to review the objectives in teams. The expected payoffs are that participants will know what learning is expected; they will be reminded of their responsibility to reach each learning objective; they will reinforce their learning for each objective; and they will develop a set of resources among their colleagues that will further support their learning. Once the team has verified the payoffs that it expects to obtain from its solutions, then it can take action with confidence.

Comments and Questions:

5. *Act, check, modify.* The final step is to put the solutions into action and then check regularly to find out if the anticipated payoffs are being realized.

Comments and Questions:

Task 4   Work as a team and review the Structured Problem-Solving Process above. As you discuss the process, give examples of what might be done at each step in the process.

Task 5   Bring any unresolved questions that you have about the Structured Problem-Solving Process to the general session for discussion.

Task 6   Read the following instructions carefully.

Instructions for Team Members

In this activity, you are to be yourselves, that is, members of the team in this workshop. One of your team members will serve as a coach and teach the team the steps in the Structured Problem-Solving Process. At the end of the practice interaction, complete the Activity 4.4 Observation Form. Designate one member to serve as the coach who will teach the team how to use the Structured Problem-Solving Process and another member as the timer. The coach will start the session.

Instructions for Designated Coach

Your goal is to use all of the general coaching skills that you have identified and the special skills of Process 1: Responding to Needs to help team members understand how to use the Structured Problem-Solving Process.

Instructions for Timer

Stop the interaction at the designated time. During the interaction, complete the Activity 4.4 Observation Form while observing the designated coach in action.

At the end of the practice interaction, lead the feedback discussion, using the Activity 4.4 Observation Form.

Task 7   Use the sequence below to conduct the activity.

1. Conduct practice interaction. *Timer:* Limit the interaction to *exactly* ten minutes.

2. Timer and members complete the Activity 4.4 Observation Form.

3. Timer leads five-minute discussion based on the Activity 4.4 Observation Form.

Task 8   Discuss the activity as a team and identify three key learning points. What did you learn from doing the activity? What would you like to remember to help you coach a team and help members interact with one another and with you? Put your key learning points on flip-chart paper and bring them to the general session for further discussion.

Activity 4.4 Observation Form

Record your observations and comments below.

1. How clearly did the coach set expectations about what the team was going to do? If you had been the coach, what would you have done differently?

2. How well did the coach use the general coaching skills to respond to the needs of the team during the process of teaching the structured problem-solving process?

   Attending

   Acknowledging

   Probing

   Reflecting

   Indicating respect

   Self-disclosure

   Immediacy

   Summarizing

Activity 4.4 Observation Form (cont.)

If you had been the coach, what would you have done differently?

3. How well did the coach use the special skills associated with Phase III: Resolving?

Reviewing: Going over key points of session to ensure common understanding

Planning: Building strategies and agreeing on next steps

Affirming: Commenting on a person's strengths and positive prospects

If you had been the coach, what would you have done differently?

Activity 4.5

Understanding and Practicing Opportunity Analysis

You have _____ minutes for this activity.

Purposes of Activity

- To understand "opportunity analysis"
- To practice the skills for using opportunity analysis.

Directions

Task 1   Review this activity as a team and ensure that your team understands what tasks it must complete.

Task 2   Select a recorder who will serve as the spokesperson for your team.

Task 3   Work as individuals and review the description of opportunity analysis below. As you read, note any comments or questions that you may have.

Opportunity Analysis

Opportunity analysis is a very powerful activity consisting of the following steps:

1. Review the systems under the team's control, looking for opportunities for improvement.
2. Select one of the systems and identify elements within it that could be targeted for improvement.
3. Use some information-developing and decision-making tool, such as brainstorming, to decide how to approach the opportunity.
4. Select the opportunity with the highest potential payoff.

Once the opportunity has been selected, the team could use the problem-solving outline described in Activity 4.3 or a project-planning outline to build an action plan for taking advantage of the opportunity.

The figure below shows a typical system with opportunities to improve team performance.

General Opportunities for Team Improvement

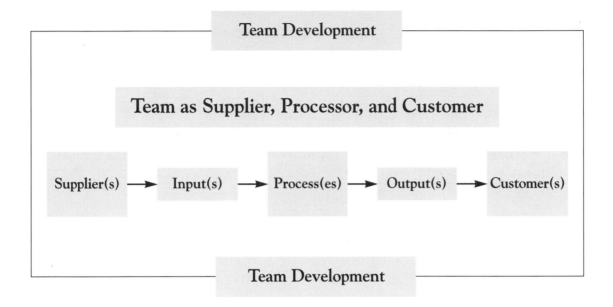

As shown in the figure, team performance is a function of *team development*, that is, the quality of team meetings, internal communication and cooperation, responsiveness, and the like. Team development is an opportunity for improving team performance. One of the first steps that a coach might propose is that the team assess its current levels of development.

Teams also receive *inputs* (services and products) from internal or external *suppliers*. The quality of these services and products can always be improved in such areas as accuracy, cost, useability, reliability, and performance.

Work is accomplished in teams, as in any organization, through work *processes*. Work processes can be improved by such actions as eliminating steps, reducing the time it takes to perform steps, eliminating inspections, and improving the consistency in a process' performance.

Teams deliver *outputs* (services and products) to internal or external *customers*. The quality of these services and products can always be improved in such areas as accuracy, cost, useability, reliability, and performance. In addition, the satisfaction of customers can be addressed to measure and improve the perceptions they have of teams' services and products and the expectations they have about these services and products.

Comments and Questions:

Task 4   Work as a team and review the description that was given of an opportunity analysis. As you discuss opportunity analysis, give examples of the kinds of opportunities you would expect to find in each of the categories shown in the figure above, that is, customers, input, output, process, and suppliers.

Task 5   Bring any unresolved questions that you have about opportunity analysis to the general session for discussion.

Task 6   Read the following instructions carefully.

Instructions for Team Members

In this activity, you are to act as yourselves, that is, members of the group in this workshop. Designate one member to serve as the coach who will teach the team how to use opportunity analysis and the steps in the process. Also designate a timer for the activity. At the end of the practice interaction, complete the Activity 4.5 Observation Form. The coach will start the session.

Instructions for Designated Coach

Your goal is to use all of the general coaching skills that we have identified and the special skills of Process 1: Responding to Needs to help team members understand how to use opportunity analysis.

Instructions for Timer

Stop the interaction at the designated time. During the interaction, complete the Activity 4.5 Observation Form while observing the designated coach in action. At the end of the practice interaction, lead the feedback discussion, using Activity 4.5 Observation Form.

Task 7 Use the sequence below to conduct the activity.

1. Conduct practice interaction. *Timer:* Limit the session to *exactly* ten minutes.
2. Timer and members complete the Activity 4.5 Observation Form.
3. Timer leads five-minute discussion based on the Activity 4.5 Observation Form.

Task 8 Discuss the activity as a team and identify three key learning points. What did you learn from doing the activity? What would you like to remember to help you coach a team and help members interact with one another and with you? Put your key learning points on a piece of flip-chart paper and bring it to the general session for further discussion.

Activity 4.5 Observation Form

Record your observations and comments below.

1. How clearly did the coach set expectations about what the team was going to do? If you had been the coach, what would you have done differently?

2. How well did the coach use the general coaching skills to respond to the needs of the team during the process of teaching the structured problem-solving process?

   Attending

   Acknowledging

   Probing

   Reflecting

   Indicating respect

   Self-disclosure

   Immediacy

   Summarizing

Activity 4.5 Observation Form (cont.)

If you had been the coach, what would you have done differently?

3. How well did the coach use the special skills associated with Phase III: Resolving?

   Reviewing: Going over key points of session to ensure common understanding

   Planning: Building strategies and agreeing on next steps

   Affirming: Commenting on a person's strengths and positive prospects

   If you had been the coach, what would you have done differently?

Activity 4.6

Critique of Video Team Coaching
Behavior Model: Process 1: Responding to Needs

You have _____ minutes for this activity.

Purposes of the Activity

- To critique a video behavior model demonstrating the process and skills of team coaching using Coaching Process 1: Responding to Needs
- To develop further the ability to recognize and use Process 1 when coaching teams

Directions

Task 1   Review this activity as a team and ensure that your team understands what tasks it must complete.

Task 2   You will observe a team coach demonstrating the process and skills of Coaching Process 1: Responding to Needs. The person on video who assumes the function of coach is Alex. You are not evaluating the total performance of this person. Your goal is to develop your ability to apply Coaching Process 1 to teams.

Think of the person on the videotape as one of your colleagues in this workshop. When you discuss what you have observed, use your discussion as an opportunity for practicing feedback. Remember that effective feedback

- Is specific and concrete
- Is descriptive of behavior (what you see and hear)
- Is free of opinion and interpretation
- Offers practical recommendations for improvement

Task 3   Read through the following material and then work as a team to review the Activity 4.6 Observation Form. Make sure that each person understands how to use the form and understands the stages and the skills noted on the form.

Task 4   Observe the video model as you complete your Activity 4.6 Observation Forms.

Task 5   After reviewing the video and completing the forms, discuss your observations as a team. Note any significant disagreements among team members and try to reconcile these disagreements.

Comments and Questions:

Task 6   Bring the results from Task 5 to the general session for discussion.

Activity 4.6 Observation Form

How often and/or how well did the coach use the following general information-developing skills? If you had been the coach, what would you have done differently?

Skill	Frequency	Quality/Notes/Comments
Attending		
Acknowledging		
Open Probes		
Closed Probes		
Reflecting		
Indicating Respect		
Self-Disclosure		
Immediacy		
Summarizing		

Activity 4.6 Observation Form (cont.)

How often and/or how well did the coach use the following process-specific skills?

Skill	Frequency	Quality/Notes/Comments
Process Stage I: *Involving*		
Clarifying		
Process Stage II: *Developing*		
Resourcing		
Confirming		
Process Stage III: *Resolving*		
Reviewing		
Planning		
Affirming		

Practice Team Coaching with Process 1: Responding to Needs

You have _____ minutes for this activity.

Purposes of Activity

- To practice coaching teams using Process 1 and its skills in a video-taped interaction
- To obtain feedback about your use of Process 1 and its skills for coaching teams

Directions

This activity can be repeated for as many iterations as there are team members. Your trainer will assign a time and the number of iterations.

Task 1 Review this activity as a team and ensure that your team understands what tasks it must complete.

Task 2 Select a recorder who will serve as the spokesperson for your team.

Task 3 Prepare for the practice interaction that follows by assigning each member of your team a letter on the table below.

Designation Letter	Team Member
A	
B	
C	
D	

Designation Letter	Team Member
E	
F	

Task 4   During this practice interaction, each team member will practice using Process 1 and its skills while coaching the team. The goal of the person functioning as a coach is to show that he or she has the discipline to use the process and skills while coaching a team. The person designated as "initiator" on the team begins the interaction by starting to tell the coach about the problem. Read and be sure that you understand the following information.

During each interaction, one team member will be designated as timer. All members (including the timer) will serve as observers and, at the end of each interaction, will use the Activity 4.7 Observation Form to give feedback to the member serving as responder (coach). The sequence for the interaction is as follows:

1. Members A (initiator) and B (responder) practice interaction. Interaction is taped and observers record their observations of responder, using the Activity 4.7 Observation Form. Taping is stopped by timer.

2. Timer leads a discussion of the interaction and observers use the observations they recorded on the Activity 4.7 Observation Form to give feedback to the person functioning as the coach.

3. Replay tape. Responder uses Activity 4.7 Observation Form to record observations of his or her own behavior. Other members verify what they have recorded on their observation forms to improve their own observation skills.

4. Repeat sequence outlined in Steps 1 through 3 until each member has functioned as the responder.

Agree as a team on a problem to be used during the interaction. You can create your own or select one of the following:

- Your team is a process improvement team. It has just begun to meet and members have decided to devote time to team development. Team members are trying to decide what to do next and seem unsure what development means. The designated coach is a member of the team. The initiator begins the interaction by saying: "I don't think any of us has a clue what team development means. If it means trying to make us be 'lovey dovey,' I'm sure not interested in wasting my time." The person who is the coach makes an appropriate response and begins the problem-solving conversation with the team.

- The team is part of a small publishing company that publishes a wide variety of self-help books. The company owners have decided that they must develop a strategy for finding market share in the field of leadership training. The team has been asked to decide how to start. The initiator begins the interaction by saying: "I think it's a dumb thing to even try to break into the training materials market. It already has too many players." The person who is the coach makes an appropriate response and begins the problem-solving conversation with the team.

- The team is part of a large retail chain and is responsible for recommending to its parent company how to reduce the steps involved in responding to employees' requests for travel documents and funds. The initiator begins the interaction by saying: "I think we just start trusting people and give them a company credit card. Let each person make his or her own plans and pay for the cost with the card. That way we could get rid of the travel office all together." The person who is the coach makes an appropriate response and begins the problem-solving conversation with the team.

- The team is a maintenance crew for the installation of a large federal agency. The team is experiencing a lot of conflict between more experienced hands (carpenters, electricians, and so on) and less experienced ones. The team leader has called a meeting to investigate the problem. The initiator begins the interaction by saying: "We are always going to have conflict if some members of this team don't get off their dead behinds and start learning how to do their jobs. Nobody wet-nursed me! I learned what I needed to know without anyone's help, and I expect the same from the people I work with when we are assigned a job." The person who is the coach makes an appropriate response and begins the problem-solving conversation with the team.

Time per Round

Ten minutes for interaction; five minutes for feedback; ten minutes for replay.

· ·

Task 5 Follow the schedule below to complete your round of practice interactions. The letter with the asterisk denotes the timer for each round. *Timers:* Stop each interaction *exactly* at the end of ten minutes.

Initiator	Responder	Observer/Timer
A	B	C, D, E, F*
B	C	D, E, F, A*
C	D	E, F, A, B*
D	E	F, A, B, C*
E	F	A, B, C, D*
F	A	B, C, D, E*

Task 6 Discuss the activity as a group and identify three key learning points. What did you learn from doing the activity? What would you like to remember? Put your three key learning points on flip-chart paper and bring them to the general session for further discussion.

Activity 4.7 Observation Form

• •

Person Observed: _____

How often and/or how well did the coach use the following general information-developing skills? If you had been the coach, what would you have done differently?

Skill	Frequency	Quality/Notes/Comments
Attending		
Acknowledging		
Open Probes		
Closed Probes		
Reflecting		
Indicating Respect		
Self-Disclosure		
Immediacy		
Summarizing		

Activity 4.7 Observation Form (cont.)

How often and/or how well did the coach use the following process-specific skills?

Skill	Frequency	Quality/Notes/Comments
Process Stage I: *Involving*		
Clarifying		
Process Stage II: *Developing*		
Resourcing		
Confirming		
Process Stage III: *Resolving*		
Reviewing		
Planning		
Affirming		

Activity 4.7 Observation Form

Person Observed: _____

How often and/or how well did the coach use the following general information-developing skills? If you had been the coach, what would you have done differently?

Skill	Frequency	Quality/Notes/Comments
Attending		
Acknowledging		
Open Probes		
Closed Probes		
Reflecting		
Indicating Respect		
Self-Disclosure		
Immediacy		
Summarizing		

Activity 4.7 Observation Form (cont.)

How often and/or how well did the coach use the following process-specific skills?

Skill	Frequency	Quality/Notes/Comments
Process Stage I: Involving		
Clarifying		
Process Stage II: Developing		
Resourcing		
Confirming		
Process Stage III: Resolving		
Reviewing		
Planning		
Affirming		

Activity 4.7 Observation Form

Person Observed: _____

How often and/or how well did the coach use the following general information-developing skills? If you had been the coach, what would you have done differently?

Skill	Frequency	Quality/Notes/Comments
Attending		
Acknowledging		
Open Probes		
Closed Probes		
Reflecting		
Indicating Respect		
Self-Disclosure		
Immediacy		
Summarizing		

Activity 4.7 Observation Form (cont.)

··

How often and/or how well did the coach use the following process-specific skills?

Skill	Frequency	Quality/Notes/Comments

Process Stage I:
  Involving

Clarifying

Process Stage II:
  Developing

Resourcing

Confirming

Process Stage III:
  Resolving

Reviewing

Planning

Affirming

Activity 4.7 Observation Form

Person Observed: _____

How often and/or how well did the coach use the following general information-developing skills? If you had been the coach, what would you have done differently?

Skill	Frequency	Quality/Notes/Comments
Attending		
Acknowledging		
Open Probes		
Closed Probes		
Reflecting		
Indicating Respect		
Self-Disclosure		
Immediacy		
Summarizing		

Activity 4.7 Observation Form (cont.)

How often and/or how well did the coach use the following process-specific skills?

Skill	Frequency	Quality/Notes/Comments
Process Stage I: *Involving*		
Clarifying		
Process Stage II: *Developing*		
Resourcing		
Confirming		
Process Stage III: *Resolving*		
Reviewing		
Planning		
Affirming		

Activity 4.7 Observation Form

Person Observed: _____

How often and/or how well did the coach use the following general information-developing skills? If you had been the coach, what would you have done differently?

Skill	Frequency	Quality/Notes/Comments
Attending		
Acknowledging		
Open Probes		
Closed Probes		
Reflecting		
Indicating Respect		
Self-Disclosure		
Immediacy		
Summarizing		

Activity 4.7 Observation Form (cont.)

How often and/or how well did the coach use the following process-specific skills?

Skill	Frequency	Quality/Notes/Comments
Process Stage I: *Involving*		
Clarifying		
Process Stage II: *Developing*		
Resourcing		
Confirming		
Process Stage III: *Resolving*		
Reviewing		
Planning		
Affirming		

Activity 4.7 Observation Form

Person Observed: _____

How often and/or how well did the coach use the following general information-developing skills? If you had been the coach, what would you have done differently?

Skill	Frequency	Quality/Notes/Comments
Attending		
Acknowledging		
Open Probes		
Closed Probes		
Reflecting		
Indicating Respect		
Self-Disclosure		
Immediacy		
Summarizing		

Activity 4.7 Observation Form (cont.)

How often and/or how well did the coach use the following process-specific skills?

Skill	Frequency	Quality/Notes/Comments
Process Stage I: *Involving*		
Clarifying		
Process Stage II: *Developing*		
Resourcing		
Confirming		
Process Stage III: *Resolving*		
Reviewing		
Planning		
Affirming		

Review and Action Log

. . . .

Record below the learning points and insights you gained from this module. Next, record ways that you might begin to apply your learning and insights and ways that you can continue to practice what you have learned.

Learning Points/Insights	Plans for Practice and Use

Module Four: Key Learning Points

1. Coaching teams requires at least three sets of skills, in addition to all the skills associated with Coaching Process 1 and Coaching Process 2:

   - Knowledge and skills to help teams structure themselves for effective team meetings
   - Knowledge and skills to manage interactions among team members
   - Knowledge and skills to help teams use the basics of team problem solving and decision making

2. Two of the most obvious and effective elements in structuring a team meeting are

   - Ensuring that the team develops and uses a clear set of norms to govern how members interact
   - Ensuring that the team is always clear and conscious about its tasks and goals

3. Knowledge and skills to manage interactions among team members include

   - Helping team members build on one another's input
   - Testing to ensure understanding
   - Keeping all members involved

4. Teams and coaches of teams need to be familiar with the following basic methods of team problem solving and decision making:

   - Structured problem-solving process
   - Opportunity analysis
   - Brainstorming
   - Nominal group technique